Clever Knits

Clever Knits

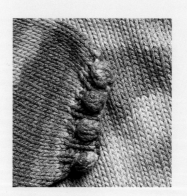

Kristine Clever

GREAT LOOKS FOR KIDS

Martingale™
& COMPANY

Credits

PRESIDENT · *Nancy J. Martin*
CEO · *Daniel J. Martin*
PUBLISHER · *Jane Hamada*
EDITORIAL DIRECTOR · *Mary V. Green*
MANAGING EDITOR · *Tina Cook*
TECHNICAL EDITOR · *Karen Costello Soltys*
COPY EDITOR · *Liz McGehee*
DESIGN DIRECTOR · *Stan Green*
ILLUSTRATOR · *Robin Strobel*
COVER AND TEXT DESIGNER · *Trina Stahl*
PHOTOGRAPHER · *Brent Kane*

Clever Knits: Great Looks for Kids
© 2002 by Kristine Clever

Martingale & Company
20205 144th Avenue NE
Woodinville, WA 98072-8478 USA
www.martingale-pub.com

Printed in Hong Kong
07 06 05 04 03 02   8 7 6 5 4 3 2 1

The information in this book is presented in good faith, but no warranty is given nor results guaranteed. Since Martingale & Company has no control over choice of materials or procedures, the company assumes no responsibility for the use of this information.

Mission Statement

We are dedicated to providing quality products and service by working together to inspire creativity and to enrich the lives we touch.

Library of Congress Cataloging-in-Publication Data
Clever, Kristine
    Clever knits : great looks for kids / Kristine Clever.
        p.   cm.
    ISBN 1-56477-414-7
    1. Knitting—Patterns.   I. Title.
TT820 .C684 2002
746.43'20432—dc21
                                                    2001044955

Dedication

To my cherubs—Tate, Karolyn, and Kamille—you are the joy of my life, and your three shiny faces inspire me to create garments as beautiful as you are.

Acknowledgments

Mom and Dad, you have given me a solid foundation and supported me through all life's endeavors—I love you!

Mike and Mary Anne, thank you for all the endless hours of baby-sitting while I "worked on my book." You truly are the best in-laws.

My sister Karen, you have set a great example for me to follow; I have always looked up to you (not physically, of course) and admired your beauty inside and out.

My brothers—Bob, Ron, Rich, and Ray—you have been there for me with your encouraging words, making me strong and able to deal with many situations. Your playful teasing has always made me feel special.

Jan Stahl, thank you for introducing me to the bigwigs of the knitting world. You have brought the best people into your shop to educate your staff and patrons. I consider myself lucky to be working for a woman who is such an active promoter of knitting. I have learned so much from you.

Barb, Jean, Dana, Sandi, Lynette, Molly, Lyn, Deb, Carolyn, and Crafty Lady students, your love of knitting makes working with all of you a pleasure. You have set high standards and expectations, but are always available to offer the help and opinions I value so much. You are an awesome group and I am blessed to know you.

Bryan, thank you for all your help with the illustrations and your moral support; you are a true friend.

Barry Klein of Trendsetter Yarns, a special thank-you for getting me into the National Needlework Association trade show that one fateful Sunday morning.

Contents

The Projects

Introduction

BEGAN KNITTING when I was six years old. My Uncle John drove my cousin Carol; my older sister, Karen; and me once a week to Sears for our knitting lessons. Being a typical child, I was not as interested in learning to knit as I was in the snacks my uncle would bring us. Our instructor lacked the patience needed to teach a child, but I persevered. A few years later, I made a pair of mittens for my dad that would have fit the Jolly Green Giant. I was a loose knitter and knew nothing about gauge. As a teenager, I continued knitting by making afghans while I baby-sat; my needles kept time to the national anthem as the television stations stopped broadcasting for the day. These early learning experiences did not hinder my love for knitting, but instead gave me confidence to tackle more difficult projects.

During my college years I went on an Icelandic kick, making sweaters for everyone in my family. That was no small feat, as I have four brothers, one sister, and nine nieces and nephews. It wasn't, however, until I started working at Crafty Lady, a knitting shop in Macomb, Michigan,

that I began writing my own patterns. Pregnant with my second child and surrounded by gorgeous yarns, I got frustrated at the lack of patterns available for children. Time was becoming a rare commodity. I wanted to get the sweater off my needles and on my child while it still fit. I began designing straightforward, fashionable garments that were quick and easy to make and that required minimal finishing details.

As my children grew older and more fashion-conscious, I incorporated ready-to-wear details so their sweaters wouldn't have that dreaded "loving hands at home" look. My ten-year-old son, Tate, has been instrumental in this process, telling me what he likes and doesn't like. I know if he wears a sweater, it's a success.

My designs are not fussy, and you can easily substitute different yarns. Each pattern has a useful tip included to provide a lesson. I hope my positive approach to knitting will encourage you to experiment with a variety of yarns and patterns. Knitting is fun!

Kristine Clever

Ready, Set, Knit!

YOU'LL BE SURPRISED at how much quality knitting time you can pack into your hectic, everyday schedule if you plan ahead, have the right tools at your fingertips, and add knitting to your to-do list.

Get Ready

KNITTING, LIKE OTHER crafts and hobbies, requires special tools that are necessary to get the job done easily and effectively. I've listed all my favorites below, but don't be afraid to experiment with other specialty items. You may find that they work great for you.

Knitting Bags

WHILE THERE ARE many different styles and types of bags, I prefer fabric totes that look like large handbags or soft-sided briefcases. I take my knitting everywhere, and I want a fashionable bag that matches my outfit and shoes (well, maybe not my shoes). Bags with inside compartments to hold spare needles and patterns are helpful, too. Many companies make bags just for knitting, so visit your local yarn shop and inquire about them.

I find most first-time knitters buy bags that are too small. They either can't believe they will need a big bag or they don't like the expense of the larger models. I recommend owning both a big bag to hold several projects as well as a smaller, one-project bag. Don't despair, your bags will get used! I have a collection of different bags, and when I'm not using them for my current knitting projects, I use them to attractively store my yarn.

Some needles, like wooden ones, don't allow your knitting to slide easily. I suggest these to loose knitters to help tighten their gauge or to someone who is working with slippery yarns, such as ribbons and metallics.

Knitting Needles

KNITTING NEEDLES COME in many types. I suggest you try different needles with the yarn you are planning to use, and select the ones that are most comfortable for you. The feel of the needles in your hands is important. You can even find bendable needles, which are more comfortable for arthritic fingers.

Some needles, like wooden ones, don't allow your knitting to slide easily. I suggest these to loose knitters to help tighten their gauge or to someone who is working with slippery yarns, such as ribbons and metallics. The tips on needles vary, too. Some are blunt and some are sharper. If a yarn splits easily, I use blunt-tipped needles, and if I'm working with multiple strands of yarn at the same time, I like to use sharper-tipped needles to help pick the stitch while keeping all the strands together.

You also have a choice between straight and circular needles. I personally do not use straight needles. They get caught up in my sleeves, require more elbowroom, and can be dangerous, especially around children. To make my knitting truly portable, I prefer circular needles; I like how the weight of the project falls in my lap, and I don't have to worry about my "sticks" being used as swords by my children. Besides, have you ever sat down unsuspectingly on a couch with a knitting needle sticking out from between the cushions? Ouch! You won't have that problem with circular needles.

To do straight knitting on circular needles, cast on stitches and then take the right-hand end of the needle in your left hand. Pick up the other end of the needle with your right hand and begin knitting. When you complete the row, take the right-hand end of the needle in your left hand and pick up the other end of the needle with your right.

Knitting Notions

THE FOLLOWING IS a list of basic notions that I find invaluable. Undoubtedly, you can find many more to help you in your knitting, so go ahead and experiment to find the right tools for you. Whatever your favorite notions, I recommend putting them in a small cosmetic case before placing them in your knitting bag; it makes it easy to find what you need, saving you time and energy. I keep two fully stocked ditty bags that I transfer from one knitting tote to another. I don't want to waste precious knitting time searching for the items I know I'll need.

Crochet hooks. I carry several crochet hooks in the D to G size range to use for finishing or for picking up dropped stitches.

Markers. I like the ones that aren't continuous rounds because I can easily clip them on my knitting to keep track of rows or stitches.

Scissors. A small pair, such as 3" embroidery scissors, is mighty handy. I run a brightly colored ribbon through one handle so I can easily find them in my ditty bag and no one will pick them up by accident.

Tapestry needles. I like the blunt, curved-tip metal needles the best. The plastic style doesn't slide easily, and the eye of the needle is too large to slip easily through stitches.

Tape measure. I carry a retractable cloth tape measure. The metal ones are fine for measuring your knitting when it's flat, but you can't take body measurements with them.

Stitch gauge. These metal rulers have a 2" slot cut out to make measuring your gauge a snap, and the guide for determining needle size is a must for every knitter.

Safety pins. I like the small brass pins to hold my garments together while I'm finishing. And if I run out of stitch markers, I can use them as a backup.

Stitch holders. You'll need several stitch holders in different sizes. I recommend the double-ended ones because if you use a stitch holder with just one end that opens, inevitably your starting point will be on the opposite side of the opening.

Calculator. A small style with easy-to-read buttons is a must for figuring gauges and yardages.

Pencil and paper. Keep these handy for making note of any changes and for keeping track of where you left off.

> Most children grow taller rather than wider, so making a garment longer will increase the wearing time.

Get Set

MEASUREMENTS FOR CHILDREN'S garments are important because of their rapid rate of growth. When determining what size to make, consider the time it will take you to complete the garment and what season it's intended for. Most children grow taller rather than wider, so making a garment longer will increase the wearing time. I think nothing of rolling up sleeves and pairing a larger sweater with leggings. When the child grows, he or she will have a nice-fitting sweater that will last another season.

Of course, there are times when a fitted sweater is desired. You'll need these four basic measurements: chest, waist (use the larger of these two), length, and sleeve length. Measure the sleeve length from the center back neck, across the shoulder, and down the arm to the wrist bone. With this measurement, you can have great results on dropped shoulder, set-in, and raglan sleeves.

As a child grows in height, you can add length by cutting off the ribbing, adding more rows of knitting, then reknitting a longer ribbing. To lengthen a sweater, open the side seams and use a knitting needle one to two sizes smaller than what the sweater was knit on to pick up stitches. Working from left to right, pick up the side bar of the V in the knit stitch, following a straight row, two rows above the ribbing.

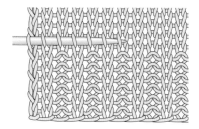

Then cut off the ribbing between the last row of ribbing and the needle. Unravel the row of knitting to the needle. You now have "live" stitches on the needle. Switch to the needle size that the sweater was knit on and knit additional rows with the yarn from the ribbing, or add a contrasting yarn to make stripes. When the sweater is the desired length before ribbing, knit the ribbing and bind off loosely.

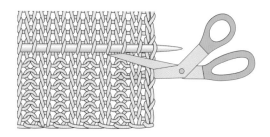

As a child grows in height, you can add length by cutting off the ribbing, adding more rows of knitting, then reknitting a longer ribbing.

For a girl's sweater, I like to knit a separate lace edging, using a complementary yarn, and attach it to the bottom edge to make the sweater longer. I'll then work a row of single crochet around the sleeve edges and neck in the same complementary yarn to pull the look together. Once you have exhausted the possibilities, it may be time to pass the sweater on to a relative or friend and make the child in your life a new favorite.

Knit!

I AM OFTEN asked how I get so much knitting done being a working, single mother of three. Working adults and stay-at-home parents are familiar with multitasking. We do it every day to make sure everything gets done. I simply include knitting with my tasks. When my children work on their homework, I sit and knit quietly beside them, ready to offer help or answer questions. The same is true for their reading time. As for *my* reading time, I enjoy listening to books on tape. They keep my hands free. And if my hands are free, I'm knitting. Another way to fit in more knitting time and keep up with your social life is to use a phone with a headset. I haven't tried this yet, but I'm thinking about it!

I carry a project with me when I take my girls to dance class and my son to his sports events. We spend a lot of time waiting at practices and rehearsals, so why not be productive? Since I am always knitting on the go, my well-stocked ditty bags are important. I knit at the doctor's office, drive-up bank, traffic jams, and even the drive-up window at McDonald's. (I am fortunate to live near one of the slowest McDonald's around.) My kids think it's a treat to go to the playland, and I don't mind obliging as long as I have a knitting project to work on. I have met a lot of curious, interesting people this way, some of whom have become my students.

I also attend several meetings a month. Nothing makes a boring or heated meeting go faster than when I take my knitting. Traveling and commuting also provide great opportunities to knit. A friend of mine lives in Chicago and takes the el to work. She uses this time to work on gauges, read new knitting books, or knit. Her long commute five days a week is enjoyable because she's doing her favorite hobby—and the gorgeous sweaters she creates make it all worthwhile.

I knit year-round. In the summer, when I take the kids to the pool, I take a smaller project like a purse or socks. This is my favorite type of multitasking—tanning and knitting!

Each of these opportunities to knit may not sound like much time, but when you add them up, you'll be amazed at how much you can get done. Check your schedule and how you can use your time and try to add more knitting. You'll be glad you did.

Finishing Techniques

THE MOST IMPORTANT technique a knitter can master is finishing. The difference between handmade and homemade is how the garment is put together. Some knitting irregularities can be hidden with proper finishing, making it well worth the time and effort to learn.

Shaping

WHEN A PATTERN says to reverse shaping, you need to change the side that the shaping was originally worked on. For example, if a decrease was done at the beginning of a knit row, the reverse would be to decrease at the end of the knit row. Bind-offs are a little different. If you bind off at the beginning of a knit row, the reverse would be to bind off at the beginning of the next row.

Blocking

I RECOMMEND BLOCKING the pieces separately before assembling. Lay out each piece and shape it to the dimensions given on the project diagram. I use a thick towel on my table, my tape measure, and T-pins to hold the pieces to the specified measurements. Set your iron on steam, and without touching your knitting, hold the iron over the piece, allowing the steam to penetrate the knitting. With your hands, flatten or shape the piece as needed, then let it dry.

Joining Shoulders: Three-Needle Bind-Off

WHILE YOU CAN bind off shoulder stitches and then sew the shoulder seams together, the three-needle bind-off method lets you join open stitches to open stitches. It makes a nice smooth join, so it's comfortable for the wearer and binding off and seaming are all done in one step.

1. Put front shoulder stitches on one needle, and back shoulder stitches on another needle; place right sides together, holding both needles in your left hand.

2. With a third needle in your right hand, insert the right needle into the first stitch on the front needle and into the first stitch on the back needle. Knit the two stitches together at the same time.

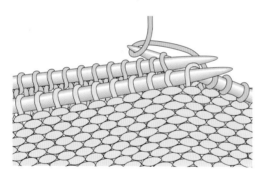

3. Repeat step 2 for a second stitch. With two stitches now on the right needle, bind off the first stitch by bringing it over the second stitch.

4. Continue knitting two stitches together (one from the front needle and one from the back needle) and binding off when there are two stitches on the right needle. When one stitch remains on the right needle, cut the yarn, leaving a short tail, and pull the tail through the last loop.

Joining Shoulders: Seaming

WHEN SHOULDER STITCHES are bound off rather than placed on stitch holders, seaming is the method used to join the pieces. Lay the two pieces right side up, with edges to be sewn butted up to each other. Working right to left, insert a threaded tapestry needle into the first V stitch on the piece nearest you, then into the V of the first stitch of the other piece. Insert the needle through both strands that make the V of the next stitch on the piece nearest you, then through the same V of the other piece. Pull just taut enough so the bound-off stitches roll to the underside of the knitting. Repeat across the shoulders, then fasten off and weave in the yarn end.

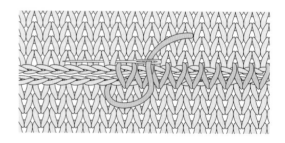

pinning the pieces together first, it will be easier to see where you'll need to pick up more bars.

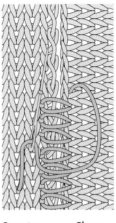

Sweater   Sleeve

Joining Sleeves to Armholes

SOME OF THE projects in this book call for you to pick up stitches around the armhole edge and knit the sleeves from the top down. In other instances, you'll need to join the sleeves to the sweater using the invisible seaming technique described here because you'll be sewing bound-off stitches to knitted rows.

With right sides up, lay the bound-off piece (sleeve) perpendicular to the edge of the row piece (armhole), and pin every 3" with safety pins. Insert a threaded tapestry needle under a stitch inside the bound-off edge (sleeve), then under one or two horizontal bars between the first and second stitches of the horizontal piece (armhole). Since there are usually more rows per inch than bound-off stitches per inch, occasionally pick up two bars on the armhole rows. By

Joining Side Seams

I JOIN SIDE seams by working on the right side of the garment. That way, I can see the finished seam and make any adjustments as I go.

1. Using safety pins, pin the pieces, wrong sides together, every 3".

2. Beginning at the lower edge, insert the needle under two horizontal bars between the first and second stitches from the edge, then under two stitches from the other edge. Pull the yarn firmly away from you; repeat, working from one side to the other. Every 3" or so, tug on the seam to make sure it isn't too tight.

Picking Up Stitches

NECKLINES AND SLEEVES are two places where you often need to pick up rather than cast on stitches. The various situations where you'd need to pick up stitches are explained below.

Horizontal edge. Use this method for picking up stitches along the back neckline. Working from right to left with the right side of the work facing you, insert the knitting needle into the first stitch in the row below the bound-off edge. Wrap the yarn knitwise around the needle and draw up a loop on the needle (one stitch picked up). Repeat across the bound-off edge.

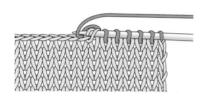

Vertical edge. Use this method for picking up stitches around armholes. Working from the bottom edge to the top with the right side of the work facing you, insert the knitting needle into the corner stitch of the first row, one stitch in from the side edge. Wrap the yarn knitwise around the needle and draw up a loop on the needle (one stitch picked up). Repeat along the edge, skipping one row every four rows to keep the edge from flaring.

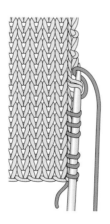

Curved edge. Use this method for picking up stitches around a shaped neckline. Working from right to left with the right side facing you, insert the knitting needle into the stitch just inside the shaped edge. Wrap yarn knitwise around the needle and draw up a loop on the needle (one stitch picked up). Neatly following the curve and hiding the jagged row-end edges, repeat around.

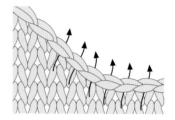

Diagonal edge. Use this method for picking up stitches around a V-neck. Working from right to left with the right side facing you, insert the knitting needle into the stitch that is one stitch in from the shaped edge, wrap yarn knitwise around the needle, and draw up a loop on the needle (one stitch picked up). Continue picking up stitches, keeping them in a straight line.

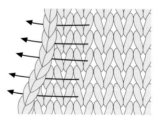

Steeking

STEEKING IS USED to create openings in garments that need to keep the continuity of the design. It's commonly used on Fair Isle patterns or other circular knitting. Essentially, you drop stitches where the opening needs to be, then cut through the center of the dropped stitches to make the opening. Here's how to do it:

1. Following the pattern instructions, bind off stitches where the opening will be.

2. With the right side facing you, work to the bound-off stitches created for the opening, cast on new stitches over the bound-off ones, and continue knitting in the pattern.

3. To create the opening, drop the same number of bound-off stitches to the bound-off edge. (Don't worry, the stitches won't drop any farther.)

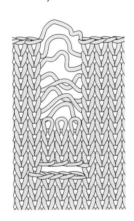

4. Cut through the center of the long bars created from the dropped stitches, and tie the ends in knots. Apply a seam sealant to the knots, let it dry, and continue with construction.

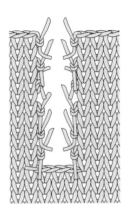

Inserting Zippers

AS A CLOSURE alternative to buttons, zippers give a sporty look to a design. If the edge that the zipper is being applied to is jagged, prepare the edge by picking up stitches and immediately binding off purlwise, or work a row of single crochet before attaching the zipper. For openings that are 6" or shorter, use a zipper that is ½" shorter than the opening. For longer openings, use a zipper that is 1" shorter than the opening. Ease the garment to the zipper to keep the seam from stretching out and giving a potbelly look.

1. Working from the right side and with the zipper closed, pin the zipper in place so the sweater edges butt up to the teeth. Make sure that both edges of the opening are even, and that the zipper starts and stops at the same place on both pieces.

2. With a needle and thread, hand sew a small backstitch one stitch in from the edge of the sweater. Turn the zipper to the wrong side and whipstitch the zipper tape in place. For a designer detail, you can stitch a narrow ribbon over the zipper tape in place of the whipstitching.

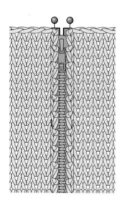 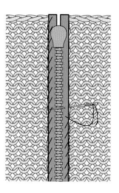

Adding Edging: Basic Crochet

SOMETIMES A CROCHETED edge provides a nice accent or finishing touch to your knitwear.

Single Crochet

WITH THE RIGHT side facing you and working from right to left, insert the crochet hook into the space between the knit stitches and draw up a loop. Wrap the yarn around the hook and draw it through the loop on the hook; *insert the hook into the next space, draw up a loop, wrap the yarn around the hook, and draw it through both loops; repeat from *. Turn, chain 1, and work the desired number of rows.

As you work the stitches, periodically check to see if the edge is lying flat. If it is rolling in or puckering, your tension is too tight. To loosen tension, either add more stitches by crocheting into the knit stitches as well as in the spaces, or switch to a larger crochet hook. If the edge is wavy, then the tension is too loose. To tighten your tension, try skipping a stitch every third stitch or switch to a smaller crochet hook.

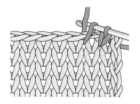 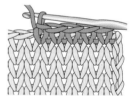

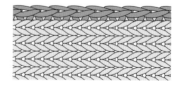

Reverse Single Crochet (Crab Stitch)

WITH THE RIGHT side facing and working left to right, insert the hook into the stitch on the right. Wrap the yarn around the crochet hook and draw up a loop. *Insert the hook into the stitch on the right, wrap the yarn around the hook, draw up a loop, then wrap and draw the yarn through both loops (stitch made). Repeat from *. Check tension as described in "Single Crochet" on page 22.

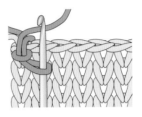

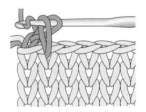

The **Projects**

I designed this sweater after attending an Instant Gratification class taught by Ann Regis. Her positive energy and anything-goes attitude moved me to create a project by combining chunky yarns on large needles. Knit with cotton yarns, this versatile tunic has been worn by my daughters as a bathing-suit cover-up, and on cooler days, over a turtleneck and leggings.

Sizes

Child's 4/6 (8/10)
Finished chest: 30" (34")
Finished length: 17" (22")

Terry Tunic

Materials

Yarn A: 4 (5) skeins of Classic Elite Sand (cotton); each skein is approx 77 yards
[308 (385) yards total]

Yarn B: 2 (3) skeins of Colinette Fandango (cotton); each skein is approx 110 yards
[220 (330) yards total]

Sizes 15 and 17 needles

Size J crochet hook

Gauge

5 sts and 7 rows = 3" in St st using 1 strand of A and 1 strand of B held together
on size 17 needles. Always check gauge before starting sweater to ensure
proper fit.

Back

1. With size 17 needles, CO 24 (28) sts, using 1 strand of A and 1 strand of B held together. Work in St st for 7 rows.

2. Work in stripe patt for 28 (38) rows.

3. Work neck and shoulder shaping:

   - P7 (8) sts, BO center 10 (12) sts; finish row. Turn work.
   - BO 7 (8) sts for shoulder.
   - Join yarn to second shoulder. BO rem 7 (8) sts.

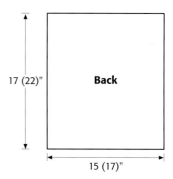

Stripe Pattern

Row 1 (WS): With 2 strands of A held together, knit across.

Row 2: Knit each st, wrapping yarns 2 times around needle.

Row 3: With 1 strand of A and 1 strand of B held together, purl across, dropping the extra wrap.

Rows 4, 5, 7, and 9: With 1 strand of each yarn, purl.

Rows 6, 8, and 10: With 1 strand of each yarn, knit.

Rep rows 1–10 for patt.

NOTE: *When switching yarns, simply carry the yarn that is not in use up the side and catch every RS row by laying yarn not in use over the working yarn before you start the row.*

Front

1. Work front the same as back to row 23 (33).

2. Work front neck shaping and shoulder shaping:

   - P9 (10) sts, BO 6 (8) sts; finish row. Turn work.
   - K9 (10) sts. Place the rem shoulder stitches on a holder. Turn work.
   - BO 1 st; finish row. Turn work.
   - K8 (9) sts. Turn work.
   - BO 1 st; finish row. Turn work.
   - BO 7 (8) sts; join yarn to second shoulder on RS neck edge, BO 1 st; finish row. Turn work.

- P8 (9) sts. Turn work.
- BO 1 st; finish row. Turn work.
- Purl across row. Turn work.
- BO 7 (8) sts.

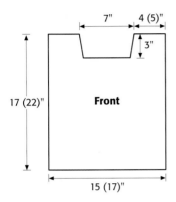

Finishing

1. Sew sleeve and side seams together, leaving 2" above hem open.

2. Hem: With size J crochet hook and 2 strands of A, work 1 row sc along bottom edges and 2" side vent openings.

3. Neckband: With size J crochet hook and 2 strands of A, work 1 row sc. On next row, work 1 round of rev sc (crab st).

4. Block the sweater, referring to page 17.

Sleeves

1. Sew shoulders together, referring to page 18.

2. From shoulder seam, measure down 6" (7") at armhole edge on the front and back; mark with safety pins.

3. With 1 strand of A and 1 strand of B held together, PU 21 (23) sts along armhole edge between the pins. Work 5 rows of St st.

4. (WS) Work rows 1–7 of stripe pattern.

5. With size 15 needles and 2 strands of A, knit 6 rows. BO.

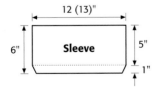

This cropped sweater is fun and fast to knit. I love the control you have on the zigzag effect of the sweater. Knit tight to make the pattern move to the left. Knit loose, and it moves to the right. You can make your "lightning bolts" as narrow or as wide as you like. The feminine touch of the bobbles softens the overall design and makes it fun for little girls to wear.

Sizes

Child's 4/6 (12/14)
Finished chest: 26" (38½")
Finished length: 12½" (16")

Note: *The yarn is space dyed to form the zigzag effect. It repeats about every fifty stitches, therefore sizing can only be done in increments of fifty stitches.*

Kaitlyn

Materials

300 (600) grams of Rainbow Mills Crayons (cotton); each 100 grams is approx
   140 yards [420 (840) yards total]
Sizes 7 and 9 circular needles, 24" long
Size 7 circular needle, 16" long
Sizes 7 and 9 double-pointed needles

Gauge

16 sts and 18 rows = 4" in St st using size 9 needles. Always check gauge before
starting sweater to ensure proper fit.

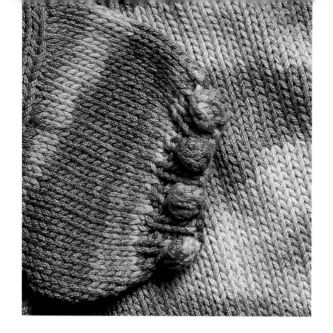

Bobble Stitch

MB IS THE abbreviation for "make bobble."

In 1 st, make 5 sts by knitting in the front and knitting in the back of the st twice, then knit in the front of the st; turn work, P5 sts; turn work, K2tog, K1, sl 1, K1, psso (3 sts); turn work, P3 sts; turn work, sl 1, K2tog, psso (1 st).

Seed Stitch

THE SEED STITCH is worked over an odd number of stitches for this sweater.

All Rows: *K1, P1; repeat from *; K1.

Body

1. With size 7 circular needles (24"), CO 90 sts (140 sts). Join, being careful not to twist sts, and place marker at beg of round.

2. First round: *(K1, P1) twice, MB; rep from *.

3. Work in K1, P1 rib for 1".

4. Inc 1 st every 9 sts [100 (150) sts].

5. Change to size 9 circular needles (24"). Knit 3 rounds, watching color to see if it stacks. It may be necessary to inc or dec 1 to 3 sts to get the yarn to make the zigzag patt. The design is determined by tension; knit loose to move the color right, and knit tight to move the color forward or to the left.

6. Work even for 6½" (9").

7. Underarms:

   • Determine front and back of sweater; mark st 50 (75) and st 100 (150).

   • Knit to 2 sts before marker, BO 4 sts; knit to 2 sts before next marker, BO 4 sts.

   • On next round, CO 4 sts over each BO.

   • Cont knitting in the round until piece measures 12½" (16").

8. Armholes:

   • Work to first underarm and steek sts (see page 21) by unraveling the 4 underarm sts down to the underarm CO. Cut and tie the ends. Rep for other underarm.

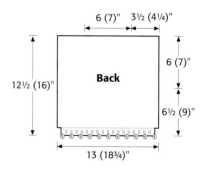

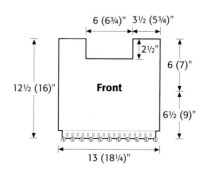

Sleeves

1. K13 (23) sts of right shoulder together using three-needle bind-off method (see page 18). For small size, leave left shoulder on a holder. For large size, join left shoulder as for right shoulder.

2. With size 9 double-pointed needles, PU 51 (57) sts. Join and place marker at beg of round. Work in St st for 1½" (3").

3. Dec 1 st before and after marker on every round 5 times [41 (47) sts].

4. Change to size 7 double-pointed needles and dec 9 sts evenly over K1, P1 rib. Cont in rib for 1".

5. MB every 4 sts, leaving an extra 0 (2) unbobbled sts at underarm. BO.

6. For large size, make left sleeve as for the right sleeve.

Front Left Shoulder, Small Size

1. Place 13 sts on size circular 9 needle. Knitting back and forth, work 2 rows of seed st.

2. Buttonhole row: Work in patt 2 sts, K2tog, YO; work in patt 4 sts, K2tog, YO; work in patt to end.

3. Work 2 more rows in seed st. BO.

Clever **Idea**

When directions specify right or left side, they're referring to the right or left side of the person who is wearing the garment.

Back Left Shoulder, Small Size

1. Place 13 sts on size 9 circular needle. Work 2 rows in seed st.

2. Bobble row: Work in patt 3 sts, MB; work in patt 5 sts, MB; work in patt 3 sts. Work 2 more rows. BO.

3. Lap front shoulder over back shoulder; sew together at armhole edge. Make left sleeve as for right sleeve.

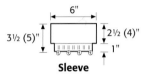

Sleeve

Neck

1. Steek 20 (25) sts of front neck down 12 rows. Place sts on a holder.

2. Beg at left back shoulder, PU 3 (0) sts from tab shoulder opening, 20 (25) sts from back neck, 7 sts down right neck, 20 (25) sts from holder, 7 sts up left neck, and 3 (0) sts on left front tab [60 (64) sts].

   NOTE: *Large size does not have shoulder opening.*

3. For small size:
   - Work in K1, P1 rib for 2 rows.
   - Row 3: K1, K2tog, YO, P1; cont in rib to last 3 sts, MB; work in patt to end.
   - Work 2 more rows of K1, P1 rib. BO loosely.

4. For large size, work 5 rounds of K1, P1 rib. BO loosely.

Finishing

BLOCK THE SWEATER, referring to page 17.

This little doll sweater is the result of playing with the stitch count for the space-dyed yarn used in the "Kaitlyn" sweater on page 31. I knew the yarn was dyed so that the color repeated every fifty stitches, so I decided to try working on just fifty stitches and see what the result would be. Turned out to be a perfect fit for my daughter's favorite 18" dolls. What little girl wouldn't love her doll to look just like her "mommy"?

Size

Fits 18" doll

Doll **Sweater**

Materials

80 grams of Rainbow Mills Crayons (cotton); 80 grams is approx 112 yards
Sizes 7 and 9 circular needles, 11" long
Sizes 7 and 9 double-pointed needles

Gauge

16 sts and 18 rows = 4" in St st using size 9 needles. Always check gauge before
starting sweater to ensure proper fit.

Body

1. With size 7 circular needles, CO 50 sts. Join, being careful not to twist sts, and place marker at beg of round.

2. Work 5 rows of K1, P1 rib. Change to size 9 circular needles. Knit every round until piece measures 4".

Underarm

1. BO 2 sts at beg of round, K23, BO 2 sts; knit to end of round.

2. On next round, CO 2 sts over the bound-off sts.

3. Work even for 1½".

Back Neck Opening

BO 1 st at center back. On next round, CO 1 st over bound-off st. Work even until piece measures 7¼".

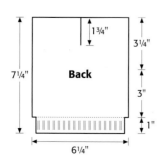

Sleeves

1. Steek sts at sides, referring to page 21.

2. Knit shoulders together using three-needle bind-off method (see page 18), with 6 sts for each shoulder. Place rem sts on a holder.

3. With size 9 double-pointed needles, PU 26 sts at armhole. Mark the beg of the round with a stitch marker.

4. Dec 1 st at beg and end of rounds every fourth row 2 times, then every third row 2 times (18 sts).

5. Work even until sleeve measures 3".

6. Dec 4 sts evenly across round. Change to size 7 double-pointed needles and work 4 rounds of K1, P1 rib. BO loosely.

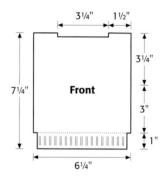

Back Neck Opening

Steek center back st. Using a sewing machine, stitch on either side of the dropped st. Cut open. Fold ends to the inside of the sweater and machine stitch in place.

Neck

1. Steek center front 11 sts down 5 rows; place sts on a holder; cut and tie ends.

2. With size 7 double-pointed needles, PU 5 sts from left back, 6 sts along left front, 11 sts from holder, 6 sts along right front, and 5 sts along right back (33 sts).

3. Work 4 rows of St st. BO loosely knitwise.

Finishing

1. Make buttonhole loop at right neck with a single loop of yarn.

2. Sew button at left neck.

3. Block the sweater, referring to page 17.

The basket-weave look of entrelac is achieved by knitting connecting diagonal squares. While it looks complicated, it's actually simple to do. As you work the entrelac pattern, you're only dealing with about ten stitches at a time, and when you finish a set, it is satisfying to see how quickly the project is growing. I used the same space-dyed yarn as in the "Kaitlyn" sweater on page 31, but here it is knitted into an interesting stripe pattern. The entrelac technique will give you lots of practice at picking up stitches. When you've finished this sweater, you'll be a pro!

Sizes

Child's 2/4 (6/8, 10/12)
Finished chest:
28" (32", 34")
Finished length:
16½" (18", 19½")

Entrelac **V-Neck Pullover**

Materials

500 (600, 700) grams of Rainbow Mills Crayon (cotton); each 100 grams is
approx 140 yards [700 (840, 980) yards total]
Sizes 7 and 9 double-pointed needles
Size 9 circular needles, 16" long
Size 7 circular needles, 24" and 16" long

Gauge

16 sts and 18 rows = 4" in St st using size 9 needles. Always check gauge before
starting sweater to ensure proper fit.

Entrelac Pattern

Foundation triangles: *K2; turn, P2; turn, K3; turn, P3. Cont in this manner, working 1 more st every RS row until 9 (10, 11) sts have been worked. Leave sts on right-hand needle; rep from * across row.

Foundation triangles

Right-side triangle: K2; turn, P2; turn, inc 1 st in first st, skpo (sl 1, K1, psso); turn, P3; turn, inc 1 st in first st, K1, skpo; turn, P4; turn, inc 1 st in first st, K2, skpo; turn, P5; turn, inc 1 st in first st, K3, skpo; turn, P6; turn, inc 1 st in first st, K4, skpo; turn, P7; turn, inc 1 st in first st, K5, skpo; turn, P8; turn, inc 1 st in first st, K6, skpo; turn, P9; for sizes 6/8 and 10/12 continue until all sts of first rectangle are used.

Right-side triangle

Left-slanting rectangles: *PU and K9 (10, 11) sts along the side of next rectangle. Turn, P9 (10, 11) sts; turn, K8 (9, 10) sts, skpo (the knit st is the first st of the next rectangle); turn, P9 (10, 11) sts; turn, K8 (9, 10) sts, skpo; cont until all sts from this rectangle are used; rep from * across row.

Left-slanting rectangles

Left-side triangle: PU 9 (10, 11) sts along side of last rectangle; turn, P2tog, P7 (8, 9) sts; turn, K8 (9, 10) sts; turn, P2tog, P6 (7, 8) sts; turn, cont until 1 st remains.

Left-side triangle

Right-slanting rectangles: *PU and P8 (9, 10) along edge of next rectangle plus 1 st on needle [9 (10, 11) sts on needle]; turn, K9 (10, 11) sts; turn, P8 (9, 10) sts, P2tog; turn, K9 (10, 11) sts; turn, P8 (9, 10) sts, P2tog; cont until all sts from first rectangle are used; rep from * across row.

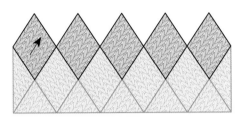

Right-slanting rectangles

Top triangles, slanting left: PU and K9 (10, 11) sts; turn, P9 (10, 11) sts; turn, K8 (9, 10) sts, skpo; turn, P7 (8, 9) sts, P2tog; cont until 1 st remains.

Top triangles, slanting left

Top half-triangle, slanting left: PU 8 (9, 10) sts plus 1 on needle; turn, P2tog; purl to end; turn, K2tog; knit to end; turn, P2tog; purl to end; cont until 1 st remains.

Top half-triangle, slanting left

Back

1. With size 7 circular 24" needles, CO 45 (50, 55) sts. Work in K1, P1 rib for 2", ending with a RS row.

2. Change to size 9 circular 24" needles. Work 5 foundation triangles.

3. Work 1 right-side triangle.

4. Work 4 left-slanting rectangles.

5. Work 1 left-side triangle.

6. Work 5 right-slanting rectangles. Steps 3–6 denote 1 set of entrelac.

7. Work steps 3–6 two more times to complete 3 sets of entrelac.

8. Work 1 top half-triangle, slanting left.

9. Work 4 top triangles, slanting left.

10. Work 1 top half-triangle, slanting left. BO last st by cutting yarn and pulling through remaining loop.

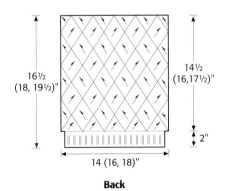

16½ (18, 19½)"

14½ (16, 17½)"

2"

14 (16, 18)"

Back

Front

1. Work front as for back until 2½ sets of entrelac are completed.

   NOTE: *A half-set ends after row 5.*

2. Beg neck shaping:
   - Work 2 right-slanting rectangles, ending on a WS row. BO off all sts except 1 on last rectangle. Cont working on right shoulder only. Place the left shoulder stitches on a holder.
   - Work 1 top triangle, slanting left. Work 1 top half-triangle, slanting left.
   - BO last st.

3. Finish neck shaping:
   - Join yarn at point A as indicated on sweater front diagram. Work 2 right-slanting rectangles.
   - Work 1 top half-triangle, slanting left, using the sts on the needle (omit the PU in the patt st directions).
   - Work 1 top triangle, slanting left. BO last st by cutting yarn and pulling through remaining loop.

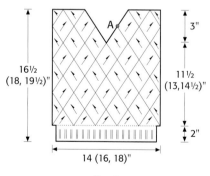

16½ (18, 19½)"

3"

11½ (13, 14½)"

2"

14 (16, 18)"

Front

Sleeves

1. Sew shoulder seams together, referring to page 18.

2. Along each side of the front and back pieces, measure down 6" (6½", 7") from shoulder seam. Mark with safety pins.

Clever **Idea**

When knitting an entrelac pattern, I recommend learning to knit backward. That way, you can eliminate purling, which involves turning your knitting every time you've completed ten or so stitches.

To knit backward, hold knitted material in your right hand, right side facing you; insert left-hand needle in back of first stitch, wrap yarn around back of left-hand needle, then toward you, and knit off; repeat across the row. It will feel awkward at first, but since you're working on only a few stitches at a time, it's worth a try.

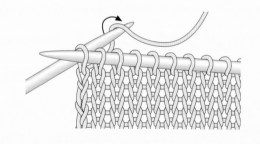

6. Change to size 7 double-pointed needles and work in K1, P1 rib for 2". BO loosely in rib.

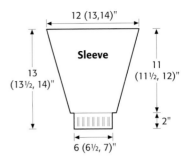

Finishing

1. With size 7 circular 24" needles, PU sts evenly around neck, making sure to PU 1 st at center point of V and place a marker before this st.

   - Row 1: Work in K1, P1 rib to 2 sts before marker, ssk; slip marker, K1, K2tog, beg with K1, rib to end of round.
   - Rep row 1 until band measures 1". BO loosely in rib.

2. Block the sweater, referring to page 17.

3. Sew side seams from rib to pins.

4. With size 9 circular needles (16"), PU 24 (26, 28) sts on both front and back [48 (52, 56) sts total]. Join and mark beg of round with a stitch marker.

5. Work in St st, knitting every round. Dec 1 st at beg and end of round every fourth round 12 (13, 14) times [24 (26, 28) sts]. Change to size 9 double-pointed needles as needed.

I love texture and dimension, but not necessarily all over a sweater. By randomly tying two-yard lengths of several different yarns together into a "magic ball," the various yarns show up intermittently as you knit the sweater. I think you'll enjoy making this project—almost as much as your little girl will enjoy wearing it. It's fun to see what fiber shows up next and how the randomness affects the look. As a finishing touch, crocheted chenille edging adds a soft touch of sweetness to the cardigan.

Sizes

Child's 2/4 (6/8, 10/12)
Finished chest: 30" (32", 34")
Finished length: 13" (15", 17")

Starlight

Materials

Yarn A: 6 (7, 8) skeins of Trendsetter Magnolia (cotton, polyurethane, acrylic, polyester, and wool); each skein is approx 55 yards [330 (385, 440) yards total]

Yarn B: 1 cone of Ironstone Cotton Chenille, approx 1000 yards

Yarn C: Using the following 4 yarns, randomly tie 2-yard lengths together and wind them into a "magic ball":

1 skein of Jacques Fonty Serpentine (polyester), approx 143 yards

1 skein of Trendsetter Charm (polyester, polyamide tactel), approx 94 yards

1 skein of Marks and Kitten Peluche (polyester), approx 73 yards

1 skein of Stahl Manuela (nylon), approx 100 yards

Size 13 needles

Size K crochet hook

Five ⅞" buttons

Gauge

9 sts and 12 rows = 4" in St st using A, B, and C held together on size 13 needles. Use a combination of yarns that knit to this gauge. Always check gauge before starting sweater to ensure proper fit.

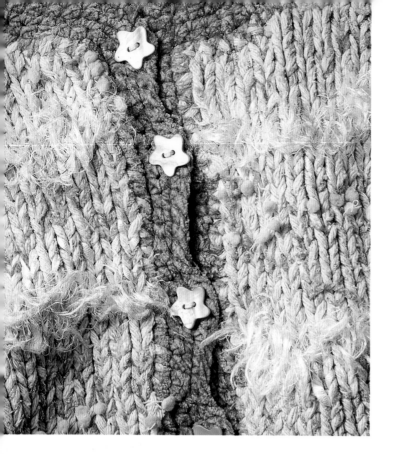

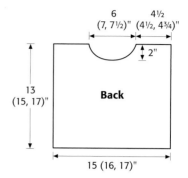

- Purl across row. Place rem 10 (10, 11) sts on a holder.

Back

1. With size 13 needles and 1 strand each of A, B, and C held together, CO 34 (36, 38) sts. Work in St st until piece measures 11" (13", 15"), ending with a WS row.

2. Work left neck shaping:

   - K12 (12, 13) sts, BO 10 (12, 12) sts; work to end. Turn work.
   - Purl across row. Turn work.
   - K1, sl 1, psso; knit to end. Turn work.
   - Purl across row. Turn work.
   - K1, sl 1, psso; knit to end. Turn work.
   - Purl across row. Place rem 10 (10, 11) sts on a holder.

3. Work right neck shaping:

   - Attach yarn to neck on WS; purl across row. Turn work.
   - Knit to last 2 sts, K2tog. Turn work.
   - Purl across row. Turn work.
   - Knit to last 2 sts, K2tog. Turn work.

Right Front

1. With size 13 needles and 1 strand each of A, B, and C held together, CO 17 (18, 19) sts. Work in St st until piece measures 10" (12", 14"), ending on a WS row.

2. Work neck shaping:

   - BO 4 sts; work to end. Turn work.
   - Work across row. Turn work.
   - BO 2 sts at neck edge; finish row. Turn work.
   - Work across row. Turn work.
   - BO 1 (2, 2) sts at neck edge; finish row. Turn work.
   - If necessary, cont until piece measures 13" (15", 17"). Place rem sts on a holder.

Left Front

1. With size 13 needles and 1 strand each of A, B, and C held together, CO 17 (18, 19) sts. Work in St st until piece measures 10" (12", 14"), ending on a RS row.

2. Work neck shaping:

   - BO 4 sts; work to end. Turn work.
   - Work across row. Turn work.
   - BO 2 sts at neck edge; finish row. Turn work.

- Work across row. Turn work.
- BO 1 (2, 2) sts at neck edge; finish row. Turn work.
- If necessary, cont until piece measures 13" (15", 17"). Place rem sts on a holder.

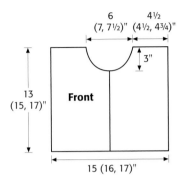

- If needed, cont until sleeve measures 10" (11", 13").
- BO rem 18 (20, 22) sts.

5. Make second sleeve the same as first.

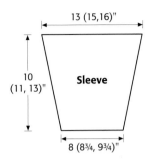

Sleeves

1. Join shoulders together using three-needle bind-off method (see page 18).

2. At outside edge, measure 6½" (7½", 8") down from shoulder seam and mark measurement with a safety pin on front and back sections.

3. With size 13 needles and 1 strand each of A, B, and C held together, PU 30 (34, 36) sts along outside edge between the pins. Work 5 rows of St st.

4. Beg sleeve shaping:
   - (RS) Dec 1 st at beg and end of every other RS row 6 (7, 7) times.

Clever Idea

The way I remember which side the buttonholes go on is this: *women* is a five-letter word, and so is *right* for right side.

Finishing

1. Front bands and neckline edging:
   - With size K crochet hook and 2 strands of B, work 2 rows of sc along right front edge, around neck, and down the left front. Work 2 sc in each of the corner sts at the center front neck edges so the band won't be too taut.
   - Using safety pins, mark the placement for 5 evenly spaced buttonholes.
   - Working a third row of sc, make buttonholes on right front by *chaining 1 st at safety pin; skip 1, then cont sc to next pin; rep from * 4 more times.
   - Work fourth row of sc, making sure to sc in the space left for the buttonhole.

2. Add scalloped edges for sleeves and sweater bottom:
   - With size K crochet hook and 2 strands of yarn B, work 1 row sc.
   - Row 2: work 1 sc; *in next st, work 3 sc; work 1 sc; rep from *.

3. Block the sweater, referring to page 17.

Many of my designs start with the yarn as the inspiration. I had my eye on the yarn I used in this sweater for some time. I loved the colors and the feel, but not the gauge. I decided to double it so I could use a larger needle. In planning the sweater, I swatched many stitches but always came back to the linen stitch. The texture of the stitch makes the colors in the tweedy yarn pop. For a totally different look, try making this vest in a solid denim-look cotton for spring and summer wear.

Sizes

Child's 4/6 (8/10, 12/14)
Finished chest:
31" (35", 40")
Finished length:
20" (22", 23")

Linen-Stitch Vest

Materials

7 (8, 11) skeins of Missoni Washington (wool, acrylic, rayon, and polyamid); each
   skein is approx 99 yards [693 (792, 1089) yards total]
   Note: If using a single strand of a bulky yarn, you will need 350 *(400, 550)* yards.
Size 10 needles
Sewing thread to match zipper
Separating zipper (see "Inserting Zippers" on page 21 to determine what length
   zipper you need)

Gauge

16 sts and 21 rows = 4" in patt st using size 10 needles. Use 2 strands of finer
yarns that knit together as one, or one bulky yarn that knits to this gauge. Always
check gauge before starting sweater to ensure proper fit.

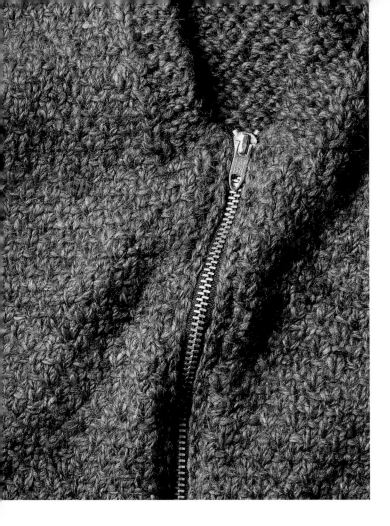

2. Beg with row 2 of patt st and work until piece measures 11" (12", 13").

3. Beg armhole shaping:

- (RS) BO 3 (4, 5) sts at beg of next 2 rows.
- Row 1 (RS): K4 sts, sl 1, K1, psso; work in patt to last 6 sts, K2tog, K4.
- Row 2: K4 sts; purl to last 4 sts, K4.
- Rep rows 1 and 2 two more times [43 (49, 55) sts].
- Cont in patt, keeping first 4 and last 4 sts in garter st until armholes measure 9" (10", 10"). Work in patt 14 (16, 19) sts, BO 15 (17, 17) sts; finish row in patt st. Place rem sts on holders.

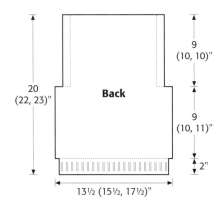

Linen-Stitch Pattern

THIS PATTERN IS always worked over an odd number of stitches.

Rows 1 and 3 (WS): Purl.
Row 2: K1, *wyif, sl 1, wyib, K1; rep from * across.
Row 4: K2, *wyif, sl 1, wyib, K1; rep from * to last st, K1.
Rep rows 1–4 for patt.

Back

1. With size 10 needles and 2 strands of yarn (or 1 strand of bulky yarn), CO 56 (64, 72) sts. Work in K2, P2 rib for 2", ending with a RS row. Work 1 more row of rib and dec 1 st so you have 55 (63, 71) sts.

Clever Idea

To ensure that front armholes measure the same as the back armholes, count how many garter ridges you have on the back outside edges and match fronts to that.

Right Front

1. With size 10 needles and 2 strands of yarn, CO 28 (32, 36) sts. Work in K2, P2 rib for 2", ending with a RS row. Work 1 more row in rib and dec 1 st [27 (31, 35) sts].

2. Starting with row 2 of patt st, work until piece measures 11" (12", 13").

3. Work armhole and neck shaping:

   - (RS) BO 3 (4, 5) sts; work in patt to last 6 sts, K2tog, K4. Turn work.
   - Work in patt across row, keeping first 4 and last 4 sts in garter st. Turn work.
   - K4, sl 1, K1, psso; finish row. Turn work.
   - K4; purl to last 4 sts, K4. Turn work.
   - K4, sl 1, K1, psso; finish row. Turn work.
   - K4; purl to last 4 sts, K4. Turn work.
   - Knit to last 6 sts, K2tog, K4. Rep this row 1 (2, 2) more times every third RS row, then 4 (5, 5) times every fourth RS row. Cont in patt on 14 (16, 19) sts until piece is the same length as back. Place sts on a holder.

Left Front

Work left front the same as right front, reversing shaping and using the following decreases: K1, sl 1, psso at outside edge and in place of K2tog at center front edge.

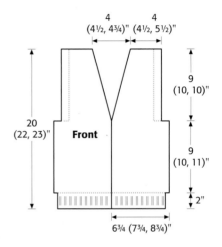

Finishing

1. Join front and back shoulders using three-needle bind-off method (see page 18).

2. With size 10 needles and 2 strands of yarn, PU 44 (47, 50) sts along right front edge. BO purlwise. Rep for left front.

3. Referring to page 21, sew zipper in by hand using a backstitch.

4. Sew side seams, referring to page 19.

5. Block the sweater, referring to page 17.

This sweatshirt is a must for every little girl. I make them one or two sizes larger than my daughters' current sizes; that way, they can roll up the sleeves and wear them with leggings and hiking boots one year and with sweatpants or jeans the next. This pattern is also a great way to try some fabulous novelty yarns because you need only a minimal amount. For younger girls, I have sewn 2"-wide lace around the perimeter of the diamond—very cute. Or, embellish the yoke with buttons, beads, or bows for an irresistible combination of cozy comfort and fashion flash!

Sizes

The finished size is determined by the size of sweatshirt you use. These directions work best on sizes 24 months to Youth Large sweatshirts.

Savvy **Sweatshirt**

Materials

Yarn A: 2 to 4 skeins of Tahki Cotton Classic; each skein is approx 104 yards
(208 to 416 yards total)

Yarn B: 2 to 4 skeins of Trendsetter Sorbet (viscose, polyester, and metallic); each
skein is approx 55 yards (110 to 220 yards total)

Good-quality raglan or set-in sleeve sweatshirt

1 skein of size 3 pearl cotton to match sweatshirt

Size 11 circular needles, 24" long

1 yard wire-edge ribbon for bow

Hand-sewing needle

Marking pencil

Gauge

12 sts and 16 rows = 4" in St st using 2 strands of A and 1 strand of B on size
11 needles. Use a combination of yarns that knit to this gauge. Always check
gauge before starting sweater to ensure proper fit.

3. Connect the marks, using a ruler and pencil, and cut off the yoke.

4. Using a tape measure and pencil, measure and mark 1" increments, ½" from the cut edge all the way around the opening.

   NOTE: *I use the width of the tape measure as a guide by laying it next to the cut edge and marking along the opposite side.*

5. With pearl cotton, sew a chain st around the cut edge, making 3 chains in each 1" space as shown.

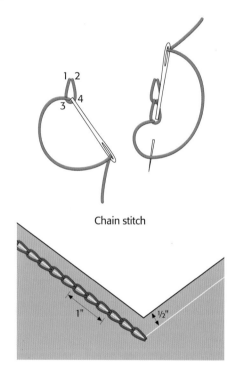

Chain stitch

Sweatshirt Preparation

1. Find the center front and center back and mark each with a pin.

2. Measure 6" down the center front, center back, and center of each shoulder or raglan sleeve and mark with a pencil.

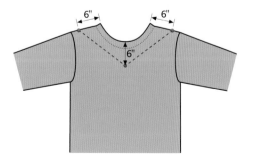

Knitting the Yoke

1. With 2 strands of A and size 11 circular needles, PU 1 st under each chain st. Place a marker on the needle at each of the 4 points: center front, center back, and center of each sleeve or shoulder. Place a different-color marker at the back point to mark beg of the round so you can easily identify it.

2. Count the sts. Be sure that the 2 front sections have the same number of sts and that the 2 back sections have the same number of sts. If necessary, make any adjustments in the first row. Note that the front sections will have more sts than the back sections because of the lower neckline.

3. (RS) Join yarn B. Purl 1 round, making any st adjustments by increasing or decreasing.

4. On the next round and every other round, work a double dec at each point marker. The double dec requires a lot of st and marker moving. However, if it is not done as described below, you will not have a straight dec line.

Double dec:

- *Purl to st before the marker, sl 1, sl marker off, sl st from right needle back to left needle, sl 2 sts together as if to knit, K1, psso. Move the finished st on right needle back to left needle, place marker on right needle, slip st back to right needle; rep from * 3 more times.
- Cont repeating rounds 1 and 2 until piece measures 4" from side of the diamond edge (not the points).

Finishing

This knitted-yoke sweatshirt looks great with either a roll neck or jewel neck.

- **Roll neck:** With 2 strands of A, knit every round on the RS for 1½". BO loosely.
- **Jewel neck:** BO loosely. With 1 strand of A, work 1 row sc and 1 row rev sc (crab st).
- **Adding a bow:** With wire-edge ribbon, make a large bow and trim ends diagonally to prevent raveling. Tack bow to sweatshirt at center-front point with thread or pearl cotton.

Block the completed yoke, referring to page 17.

Clever **Idea**

Because the prep work is time-consuming, I prepare several sweatshirts at one time. Then when I'm ready to knit, I can just pick one up and go!

I love getting cozy in my big comfy mohair-and-chenille sweater and figured my girls would enjoy the luxury, too. I added bobbles and bows to the little girl's version to make it playful and young.

The head-hugging hat emphasizes my daughters' wavy hair by allowing the wispy ends to flip up over the rolled brim. The perfect frame for perfect faces!

Sizes

Child's 4 (6, 8, 10, 12)
Finished chest: 30"
(32", 34", 36", 38")
Finished length: 15"
(16", 17", 18", 19")

Bobbles and Bows **Sweater**

Materials

Yarn A: 3 (3, 3, 4, 4) skeins of Sirdar Chenille (acrylic and nylon); each skein is approx 171 yards [513 (513, 513, 684, 684) yards total]

Yarn B: 5 (5, 5, 6, 6) skeins of Austerman Piroshka (synthetic); each skein is approx 100 yards [500 (500, 500, 600, 600) yards total]

Yarn C: 5 (5, 5, 6, 6) skeins of Ironstone Hot Stuff (mohair and acrylic); each skein is approx 105 yards [525 (525, 525, 630, 630) yards total]

Sizes 9, 13, and 15 needles

Size K crochet hook

2 yards of ¼"-wide double-faced satin ribbon

Gauge

9 sts and 14 rows = 4" in St st using 1 strand each of A, B, and C held together on size 15 needles. Use a combination of yarns that knit to this gauge. Always check gauge before starting sweater to ensure proper fit.

- Purl across row. Turn work.
- K1, sl 1, psso; finish row. Turn work.
- Purl across row. Turn work.
- BO 10 (10, 11, 11, 12) sts loosely.

4. Work right neck shaping:

- Attach 1 strand each of A, B, and C at WS of neck edge.
- Purl across row. Turn work.
- Knit to last 3 sts, K2tog, K1. Turn work.
- Purl across row. Turn work.
- Knit to last 3 sts, K2tog, K1. Turn work.
- Purl across row. Turn work.
- BO 10 (10, 11, 11, 12) sts loosely.

5. Work front the same as back.

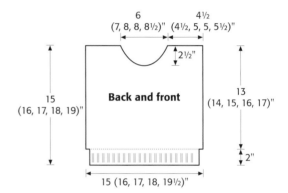

Back and Front

1. With size 13 needles and 1 strand each of A, B, and C held together, CO 34 (36, 38, 40, 43) sts. Work in K1, P1 rib for 2".

2. Switch to size 15 needles and cont in St st until piece measures 12½" (13½", 14½", 15½", 16½") from beg, ending with a WS row.

3. Work left neck shaping:

- (RS) Work first 12 (12, 13, 13, 14) sts, BO 10 (12, 12, 14, 15) sts; finish row. Turn work.
- Purl across left shoulder sts. Place right shoulder sts on a holder. Turn work.
- K1, sl 1, psso; finish row. Turn work.

Sleeves

1. Sew shoulder seams together, referring to page 18.

2. Measure 7" (7", 8", 9", 9") down from shoulder seam on front and back armhole edges; mark with safety pins.

3. With size 15 needles and 1 strand each of A, B, and C held together, PU 34 (34, 36, 40, 40) sts, spacing them evenly between pins. Work in St st for 1", ending on WS row.

4. To shape sleeve, on RS row, K2tog at beg and end every fourth row 6 (6, 7, 9, 9) times. Work even until sleeve measures 10" (11", 12", 13", 14") or desired length.

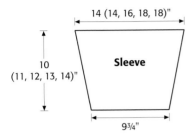

14 (14, 16, 18, 18)"

10 (11, 12, 13, 14)"

Sleeve

9¾"

Clever **Idea**

When determining what size sweater to make, always base your decision on the finished measurements, not the numerical size. Every designer has a different opinion on how much ease to add to a garment. Sometimes it's comfort ease, and other times it's design ease.

Finishing

1. Sew side and sleeve seams.

2. With size K crochet hook and 2 strands of yarn A, work 1 row of sc and 1 row rev sc (crab st).

3. With size 9 needles and 2 strands of yarn A, make 5 bobbles as follows:

   - CO 1 st.
   - Row 1: Knit in the front and back of st until 5 sts are on needle; turn work.
   - Row 2: P5; turn work.
   - Row 3: K1, sl 1, psso, K1, K2tog; turn work.
   - Row 4: P3; turn work.
   - Row 5: Sl 1, K2tog, psso; turn work.
   - Row 6: BO last st; leave tail to tie bobble onto sweater.

4. Using ribbon, tie 5 bows in assorted sizes. Randomly tack the bows and bobbles onto the sweater front.

5. Block the sweater, referring to page 17.

Bobbles and Bows **Hat**

Materials

Yarn A: 1 skein of Sirdar Chenille (acrylic and nylon); each skein is approx 171 yards

Yarn B: 1 skein of Ironstone Hot Stuff (mohair and acrylic); each skein is approx 105 yards

Sizes 9 and 10 needles

Size 9 double-pointed needles

Gauge

16 sts and 21 rows = 4" in St st using 1 strand of B on size 10 needles. Use yarn that knits to this gauge. Always check gauge before starting hat to ensure proper fit.

Sizes

Child's 4/6 (10/12)
Finished circumference:
18½", 20"

Lower Edge

1. With size 9 needles and yarn A, CO 74 (80) sts. Work in St st for 1½".

2. Change to yarn B and size 10 needles; cont in St st for 3", ending on a WS row.

Crown Shaping

1. (RS) Change to 2 strands of yarn A; knit 1 row, purl 1 row.

2. Beg decreases:
   - K1, *K10 (K11), K2tog; rep from * to last st, K1.
   - Purl all WS rows.
   - K1, *K9 (K10), K2tog; rep from * to last st, K1.
   - K1, *K8 (K9), K2tog; rep from * to last st, K1.
   - K1, *K7 (K8), K2tog; rep from * to last st, K1.
   - K1, *K6 (K7), K2tog; rep from * to last st, K1.
   - K1, *K5 (K6), K2tog; rep from * to last st, K1.
   - K1, *K4 (K5), K2tog; rep from * to last st, K1.
   - K1, *K3 (K4), K2tog; rep from * to last st, K1.
   - K1, *K2 (K3), K2tog; rep from * to last st, K1.
   - For large size only: K1 *K2, K2 tog; rep from * to last st, K1.
   - *K2tog; rep from * for 2 rows.

3. Slip rem 5 sts on size 9 double-pointed needle to make I-cord. K5, slide sts to other end of needle, K5. Cont knitting and sliding sts until I-cord is 3" long. Cut an 18" tail of yarn and thread it through the 5 sts; pull tightly.

Finishing

1. Sew the back seam with the tail of yarn. Remember to reverse stitching at lower edge because the wrong side of the brim will show when the brim rolls back.

2. Tie a knot in the I-cord to top off the hat.

With just one skein of Wool Pak yarn, I challenged myself to make a sweater for my son. I had only 430 yards, so I knew I had to bulk up the gauge in order for it to work. The search was on for a yarn to combine with it that would add color and texture. The Annabelle yarn by itself seemed feminine, but when added to the Wool Pak, the resulting mix of colors was both masculine and pleasing. Fun zipper buttons finish the look.

Sizes

Child's 4 (6, 8, 10)
Finished chest:
30" (32", 34", 36")
Finished length:
14" (16", 17", 18")

Tate's **Cardigan**

Materials

Yarn A: 1 (1, 2, 2) skeins of Wool Pak NZ 10-ply; each skein is approx 430 yards
[430 (430, 860, 860) yards total]

Yarn B: 5 (5, 7, 7) skeins of Filatura Annabelle (polyester and acrylic; each skein is
approx 93 yards [465 (465, 651, 651) yards total]

Sizes 9 and 11 needles

Size J crochet hook

Four ⅞" buttons

Stitch holders

Safety pins

Gauge

12 sts and 16 rows = 4" in St st using 1 strand of A and 1 strand of B held together
on size 11 needles. Use a combination of yarns that knits to this gauge. Always
check gauge before starting sweater to ensure proper fit.

4. Work right back neck and shoulder shaping:

   - Attach yarns at WS neck edge; BO 1 st; finish row. Turn work.
   - Knit across row. Turn work.
   - BO 1 st; finish row. Turn work.
   - Cont in St st to match left shoulder. Place rem 13 (14, 16, 17) sts on a holder.

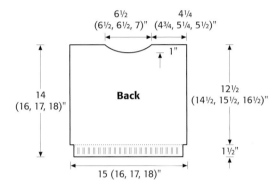

Back

1. With size 9 needles and 1 strand of A and B held together, CO 45 (48, 51, 54) sts. Work in K1, P1 rib for 1½".

2. Switch to size 11 needles and work in St st until piece measures 13" (15", 16", 17") from beg, ending with a WS row.

3. Work left back neck and shoulder shaping:

   - (RS) K15 (16, 18, 19) sts, BO 15 (16, 15, 16) sts; finish row. Turn work.
   - Purl left shoulder sts. Place right shoulder stitches on a holder. Turn work.
   - BO 1 st; finish row. Turn work.
   - Purl across row. Turn work.
   - BO 1 st; finish row. Turn work.
   - Cont in St st until piece measures 14" (16", 17", 18") from bottom. Place rem 13 (14, 16, 17) sts on a holder.

Left Front

1. With size 9 needles and 1 strand each of A and B held together, CO 21 (23, 24, 26) sts. Work in K1, P1 rib for 1½".

2. Change to size 11 needles. Work in St st until piece measures 8" (9", 9", 10").

3. Beg neck shaping: Knit to last 2 sts, K2tog. Repeat every other row 5 times, then every fourth row 3 (4, 3, 4) times.

4. Work even until front is the same length as back.

5. Place rem sts on a holder.

Right Front

WORK SAME AS left front, reversing the shaping. Sl 1, K1, psso, knit to end of row. Repeat every other row 5 times, then every fourth row 3 (4, 3, 4) times.

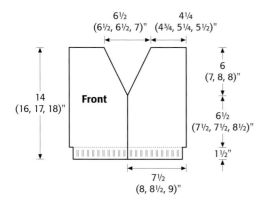

6½
(6½, 6½, 7)"   4¼
(4¾, 5¼, 5½)"

Front

14
(16, 17, 18)"

6
(7, 8, 8)"

6½
(7½, 7½, 8½)"

1½"

7½
(8, 8½, 9)"

Sleeves

1. Knit shoulders together using three-needle bind-off method (see page 18).

2. At outer edge of each shoulder seam, measure 7½" (8", 8½", 9") down from shoulder seam, and mark both front and back sections with safety pins.

Clever **Idea**

For perfect sleeve length, have the child try on the sweater after the shoulders are sewn together, and measure from the outer shoulder edge to the wrist bone. Make necessary adjustments on the pattern, then knit the sleeves.

3. With size 11 needles and 1 strand each of A and B held together, PU 45 (48, 51, 54) sts on the outer edge between pins. Work 3 rows in St st.

4. To shape sleeve, on RS row, dec 1 st at each end by K2tog. Cont to dec 1 st at each end every fourth row 9 (10, 10, 11) more times. Work even until sleeve is 1½" shorter than desired length.

5. Change to size 9 needles and work in K1, P1 rib for 1½". BO.

6. Rep steps 3–5 to make the other sleeve.

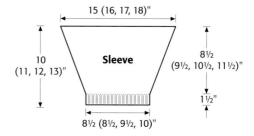

15 (16, 17, 18)"

Sleeve

10
(11, 12, 13)"

8½
(9½, 10½, 11½)"

1½"

8½ (8½, 9½, 10)"

Finishing

1. Sew side and underarm seams.

2. Front bands and neck:

   - With size J crochet hook and 1 strand each of A and B held together, work 1 row sc. Chain 1. Turn work.
   - Row 2: At left side for boys or right side for girls, work 4 buttonholes evenly spaced: sc to first buttonhole; *chain 2, skip 2, sc to next buttonhole; rep from * 3 more times.
   - Row 3: sc to buttonholes; work 2 sc in each buttonhole; finish row.

3. Sew on buttons.

4. Block the sweater, referring to page 17.

The inspiration for this Nordic-feel sweater came from the yarn. To play up the red and blue flecks in the neutral color yarn, I added a red fingering-weight yarn, which enhanced the colors without being overpowering. The whipstitch detail along the neck, bottom, and sleeve edges was part of the original plan, but I added the armhole edging out of necessity to conceal a less-than-perfect assembly job. Life is too short and children grow too fast to get hung up on details! What could have been a negative turned out to be a positive improvement on the overall design.

Sizes

Child's 4 (6, 8, 10)
Finished chest:
29" (31", 33", 35")
Finished length:
15" (17", 19", 21")

Kirsten

Materials

Yarn A: 5 (6, 7, 8) skeins of Reynolds Lopi (100% wool); each skein is approx 100 yards [500 (600, 700, 800) yards total]

Yarn B: 3 (4, 4, 5) skeins of Stahl Linda (100% cotton); each skein is approx 186 yards [558 (744, 744, 930) yards total]

Size 10 needles

Size 9 circular needles, 16" long

Gauge

12½ sts and 16 rows = 4" in St st using size 10 needles and 1 strand of A and 1 strand of B held together. Use a yarn that knits to this gauge. Always check gauge before starting sweater to ensure proper fit.

- Knit across row. Turn work.
- Purl across row. Place rem 16 (16, 18, 19) sts on a holder.

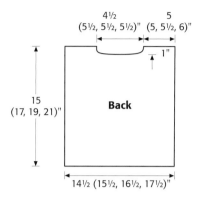

Front

1. Work front the same as back until piece measures 12" (14", 16", 18") from bottom, ending with a WS row.

2. Work right neck shaping:

   - K20 (21, 23, 24) sts, BO 5 (6, 6, 7) sts and place on a holder; finish row. Turn work.
   - Purl across right shoulder sts. Turn work.
   - BO 1 (2, 3, 2) sts; finish row. Turn work.
   - Purl across row. Turn work.
   - BO 2 sts for all sizes; finish row. Turn work.
   - Purl across row. Turn work.
   - BO 1 st for all sizes; finish row. Turn work.
   - Work even until front measures the same as back. Place rem 16 (16, 17, 19) sts on a holder.

3. Work left neck shaping:

   - Join yarn at WS neck edge, BO 1 (2, 3, 2) sts; finish row. Turn work.

Back

1. With size 10 needles and 1 strand each of A and B held together, CO 45 (48, 52, 55) sts. (RS) Purl 2 rows.

2. Knit next row and work in St st until piece measures 14" (16", 18", 20"), ending on a WS row.

3. Work left back neck shaping:

   - (RS) Work across 17 (17, 19, 20) sts and place on a holder, BO center 11 (14, 14, 15) sts; finish row. Turn work.
   - Purl across left shoulder sts. Turn work.
   - BO 1 st; finish row. Turn work.
   - Purl across row. Place rem 16 (16, 18, 19) sts on a holder.

4. Work right back neck shaping:

   - Join yarn at WS of right shoulder, BO 1 st; finish row. Turn work.

- Knit across row. Turn work.
- BO 2 sts for all sizes; finish row. Turn work.
- Knit across row. Turn work.
- BO 1 st for all sizes; finish row. Turn work.
- Knit across row. Turn work.
- Work even until front measures the same as back. Place rem 16 (16, 17, 19) sts on a holder.

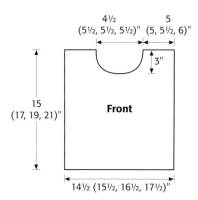

4½
(5½, 5½, 5½)"   5 (5, 5½, 6)"

3"

15
(17, 19, 21)"

Front

14½ (15½, 16½, 17½)"

Sleeves

1. With size 10 needles and 1 strand each of A and B held together, CO 26 (26, 30, 34) sts. Purl for 2 rows. Knit next row and cont in St st until piece measures 1½", ending with a WS row.

2. Beg sleeve shaping: Inc 1 st at each end every fourth row 10 (10, 10, 11) times. Cont in St st until sleeve measures 10½" (12", 14", 16") or desired length [46 (46, 50, 56) sts total].

3. BO loosely.

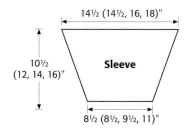

14½ (14½, 16, 18)"

10½
(12, 14, 16)"

Sleeve

8½ (8½, 9½, 11)"

Clever Idea

The number-one reason sweaters look homemade is that the sleeves fit too tightly into the armhole. When sleeves are knit separately, they need to be bound off very loosely; otherwise, the fit will be tight. If you have trouble binding off loosely, use a needle two or three sizes larger than the one you knit with when you bind off the sleeve stitches.

Finishing

1. Knit shoulders together using three-needle bind-off method (see page 18).

2. With size 9 circular needles and 1 strand each of A and B held together, PU sts evenly around neck edge. Join.

   - Round 1 (RS): Purl.
   - Round 2: Knit.
   - BO purlwise.

3. Sew sleeves to armholes, referring to page 19.

4. Sew the underarm and side seams.

5. Using a yarn needle and 4 strands of B, whipstitch around purl ridges on armhole seams and bottom, neck, and sleeve edges.

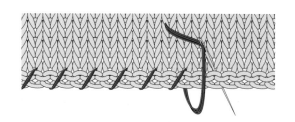

6. Block the sweater, referring to page 17.

KIRSTEN

With the popularity of polar fleece today, I wanted to design a sweater for older boys that mimicked the look and feel of that fabric. The wearing comfort and the knitting ease of this sweater are enhanced with simple tricks: The purl ridges work as faux-serged seams. And the machine-stitched label imitates ready-to-wear garments, which are much more appealing to older children than the dreaded "loving hands at home" look.

Sizes

Child's 4 (6, 8, 10, 12)
Finished chest: 32"
(34", 36", 38", 40")
Finished length:
21" (22", 23", 24", 25")

Fleece **Tunic**

Materials

Yarn A: 4 (4, 5, 5, 6) skeins of Rowan Chunky Soft (wool, acrylic, alpaca, polyamid)
    light gray; each skein is approx 60 yards [240 (240, 300, 300, 360) yards total]
Yarn B: 4 (5, 5, 6, 6) skeins of Rowan Chunky Soft dark gray; each skein is approx
    60 yards [240 (300, 300, 360, 360) yards total]
Sizes 10½ and 11 needles

Gauge

11 sts and 16 rows = 4" in St st using size 11 needles. Use a yarn that knits to
this gauge. Always check gauge before starting sweater to ensure proper fit.

4. To shape shoulders, BO 6 (7, 7, 7, 8) sts at beg of next 4 rows. Place rem sts on a holder.

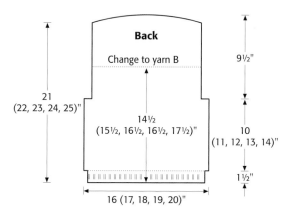

Front

1. Work front the same as back until piece measures 17½" (18", 18", 19", 19"), ending with a WS row.

2. Work 18 (20, 21, 21, 23) sts and place on a holder, BO next 2 sts; finish row. Turn work.

3. Work right neck shaping:
    • Purl across right neck sts. Turn work.
    • K1, sl 1, K1, psso; finish row. Turn work.
    • Rep last 2 rows 5 (5, 6, 6, 6) more times. Cont in St st until piece measures 20" (21", 22", 23", 24"). Place rem sts on a holder.

4. To shape shoulder, BO 6 (7, 7, 7, 8) sts at armhole edge 2 times.

5. Work left neck shaping:
    • Join yarn B on WS; purl across row. Turn work.

Back

1. With size 10½ needles and yarn A, CO 44 (48, 50, 52, 56) sts. Knit 6 rows.

2. Change to size 11 needles. Work in St st until piece measures 11½" (12½", 13½", 14½", 15½").

3. Beg armhole shaping:
    • BO 3 (3, 3, 4, 4) sts at beg of next 2 rows. Cont in St st until piece measures 14½" (15½", 16½", 16½", 17½"), ending with a WS row.
    • (RS) Change to yarn B. Knit 2 rows. Work in St st with yarn B until piece measures 20" (21", 22", 23", 24").

- Knit to last 3 sts, K2tog, K1. Rep last 2 rows 5 (5, 6, 6, 6) more times. Finish as for right shoulder.

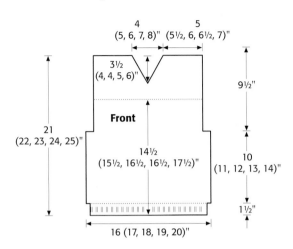

Sleeves

1. Join shoulders using three-needle bind-off method (see page 18).

2. With size 11 needles and yarn B, PU 46 (46, 46, 52, 52) sts on straight edge of armhole, not along underarm bound-off sts.

3. (WS) Knit 1 row to form ridge.

4. Work 2" in St st, then begin sleeve shaping:
   - Dec 1 st at each end of every 4th row 10 times [26 (26, 26, 32, 32) sts].
   - Cont until sleeve measures 13½" (14½", 15½", 16½", 17½") or desired length.
   - Change to size 10½ needles and knit 6 rows. BO loosely.

5. Rep steps 1–4 to make second sleeve.

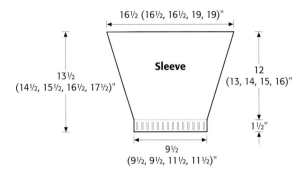

Finishing

1. Sew underarm bind-offs to upper sleeve edges, referring to page 19.

2. Sew sleeve seams. Sew side seams from sleeves to garter ridge; leave ridge portion open for a tunic style.

3. Sew in yarn tails along neck to form an even V-neck edge.

4. Machine stitch a label to left front just above ridge.

5. Block the sweater, referring to page 17.

Clever **Idea**

For a ready-to-wear look, order custom-made labels with your name or a fun nickname on them, and machine stitch them onto garments. You can usually order labels from your local yarn shop or from mail-order sources listed in knitting magazines.

My daughter's dream coat was created from her specifications. She picked the colors and decided where she wanted them. I wanted the tassels as the focus, so I exaggerated that design detail. Just because children are small doesn't mean that the details have to be small. I learned from knitwear designer and author Laura Bryant that an exceptional design is created by adding the unexpected. If you're making this coat for an older child, you may want to omit the tassels and try adding a purchased decorative zipper pull instead.

Sizes

Child's 4/6 (8/10, 12/14)
Finished chest:
32" (34", 36")
Finished length:
22" (24", 26")

Kamille's Color-Blocked **Coat**

Materials

Yarn A: 6 (7, 8) skeins of Reynolds Lopi (100% wool); each skein is approx 100 yards
[600 (700, 800) yards total] for fronts, back, cuffs, and hood trim

Yarn B: 2 (3, 3) skeins of Reynolds Lopi (100% wool); each skein is approx 100 yards [200 (300, 300) yards total] for sleeves

Yarn C: 2 (3, 3) skeins of Reynolds Lopi (100% wool); each skein is approx 100 yards [200 (300, 300) yards total] for hood

Sizes 9 and 10 needles

16" (18", 20") separating zipper

Gauge

14 sts and 18 rows = 4" in St st using size 10 needles. Use a yarn that knits to this gauge. Always check gauge before starting sweater to ensure proper fit.

3. To shape armhole, BO 4 sts at beg of next 2 rows 50 (52, 56) sts.

4. Cont St st until piece measures 22" (24", 26") from lower edge.

5. BO loosely.

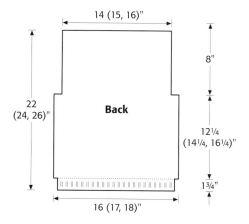

Seed Stitch

THE SEED STITCH is worked over an even number of stitches for this sweater.

Row 1 (RS): *K1, P1; repeat from * to end.
Row 2: *Pl, K1; repeat from * to end.

Back

1. With size 9 needles and yarn A, CO 58 (60, 64) sts. Work in seed st for 8 rows.

2. Change to size 10 needles. Work in St st until piece measures 14" (16", 18").

Left Front

1. With size 9 needles and yarn A, CO 28 (30, 32) sts. Work in seed st for 8 rows.

2. Change to size 10 needles. Work in St st until piece measures 14" (16", 18"), ending with a WS row.

3. To shape armholes, BO 4 sts. Cont in St st until piece measures 20" (22", 24"), ending with a RS row.

4. Work neck shaping:

   • (WS) BO 5 sts; finish row. Turn work.

   • Knit across row. Turn work.

   • BO 1 st; finish row. Turn work. Rep last 2 rows 2 more times 16 (18, 20) sts.

   • If needed, cont in St st until front is same length as back. BO loosely.

Right Front

WORK SECOND FRONT the same as first, but reverse all shaping.

1. (WS) To shape armholes, BO 4 sts. Cont in St st until piece measures 20" (22", 24"), ending with a WS row.

2. Work neck shaping:

   - (RS) BO 5 sts; finish row. Turn work.
   - Purl across row. Turn work.
   - BO 1 st; finish row. Turn work. Rep last 2 rows 2 more times 16 (18, 20) sts.
   - If needed, cont in St st until front is same length as back. BO loosely.

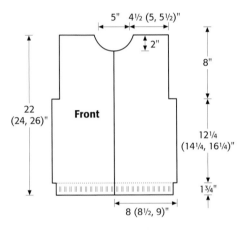

Clever Idea

When sewing embellishments, such as buttons or tassels, onto sweaters, use size 3 pearl cotton. It's stronger than sewing thread and you don't have to reinforce as many times.

Sleeves

1. With size 9 needles and yarn A, CO 40 (42, 44) sts. Work in seed st for 8 rows.

2. Change to size 10 needles and yarn B. Work in St st for 4 rows.

3. Work sleeve shaping:

   - Inc 1 st at each end every fourth row 8 (7, 6) times (56 sts).
   - Work even in St st until sleeve measures 14" (15", 16") from beg or desired length.
   - BO loosely.

4. Rep steps 1–3 to make second sleeve.

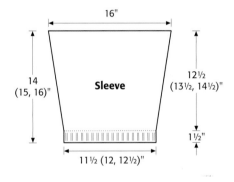

Clever **Idea**

When you let your child participate in the design process, you're much more likely to create a garment that he or she will love to wear. My daughter chose the colors for this project and decided where each should go, and she just loves her coat.

Hood

1. With size 9 needles and yarn A, CO 76 sts. Work in seed st for 6 rows.

2. Change to size 10 needles and yarn C. Work in St st for 6" or until piece measures about 7".

3. Beg right hood shaping:

   - (RS) Knit across 37 sts, BO 2 sts; finish row. Turn work.
   - Purl to BO. Turn work.
   - BO 1 st; finish row. Turn work.
   - Purl across row. Turn work.
   - BO 1 st; finish row. Turn work.
   - BO loosely.

4. Left hood shaping:

   - Join yarn C at center back on WS, BO 1 st; finish row. Turn work.
   - Knit across row. Turn work.
   - BO 1 st; finish row. Turn work.
   - Knit across row. Turn work.
   - Purl across row. Turn work.
   - BO loosely.

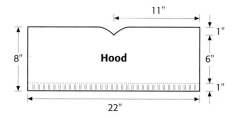

Finishing

1. With size 9 needles and yarn A, PU 82 sts along front bands. Work 6 rows in seed st. BO knitwise.

2. Sew shoulder seams, referring to page 18.

3. Sew hood seam. Attach hood to neckline, matching center backs and spacing hood evenly along neckline.

4. Sew sleeves to armholes, then sew side and underarm seams.

5. Using a backstitch, sew zipper to sweater fronts, starting 5" from bottom edges. Be sure to ease fronts to zipper so zipper will lie flat.

6. Block the sweater, referring to page 17.

Clever **Idea**

For a smoother edge when binding off, don't work the first stitch. Instead, slip it to the right needle, work one stitch, then bind off.

My son, Tate, has a fleece pullover with a stand-up collar that he told me was "cool." His comment planted the idea for the basic design in my mind. Then our shopping trip to pick out the yarn solidified the sweater. He was rather picky about the feel of the yarn and the color. Knowing green is his favorite color, I was surprised—and thrilled—when he chose the rich bronzy tone. Since ribbed sweaters are popular, I used a mock-rib stitch to give a similar look without the clinginess.

Sizes

Youth 8 (12, 16)
Finished chest:
32" (36", 40")
Finished length:
20" (22½", 25")

Zippered **Pullover**

Materials

7 (8, 10) skeins of Sirdar Super Nova (wool, acrylic); each skein is approx 124
   yards [868 (992,1240) yards total]
Sizes 10 and 10½ needles
7" metal nonseparating zipper
Size G crochet hook

Gauge

12½ sts and 16 rows = 4" in patt st using size 10½ needles. Use a bulky yarn
that knits to this gauge. Always check gauge before starting sweater to ensure
proper fit.

Mock-Rib Stitch

NOTE: *This stitch must be done in a multiple of 7 plus 2 sts.*

Row 1 (RS): Knit.
Row 2: K2, *P5, K2; rep from * across row.

Back

1. With size 10½ needles, CO 51 (58, 65) sts. Work in patt st until piece measures 12" (14", 16").

2. BO 4 (5, 5) sts at beg of next 2 rows to shape armhole [43 (48, 55) sts].

3. Cont until armhole measures 8" (8½", 9"). Place rem sts on a holder.

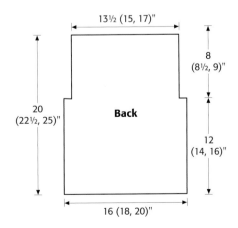

Front

1. Work front the same as back until armhole measures 2½".

2. Beg zipper opening:
   - Work first 21 (23, 26) sts, BO center 1 (2, 3) sts; finish row. Turn work.
   - Work in patt st until you reach bound-off st(s). Place rem sts on a holder. Turn work.
   - Cont working one side of zipper opening until armhole measures 5" (5½", 6"), ending with a WS row.

3. Beg neck shaping:
   - (RS) BO 3 (3, 4) sts at neck edge; finish row. Turn work.
   - Work across row. Turn work.
   - BO 3 (3, 4) sts at neck edge; finish row. Turn work.
   - Work across row. Turn work.
   - BO 2 (2, 3) sts at neck edge; finish row. Turn work.
   - Cont in patt until front is the same length as back. Place rem sts on a holder.

4. Complete neck shaping on other side of zipper opening:
   - Join yarn at neck edge on WS. Cont in patt until armhole measures 5" (5½", 6"), ending with a RS row.
   - BO 3 (3, 4) sts at neck edge; finish row. Turn work.
   - Work across row. Turn work.
   - BO 3 (3, 4) sts at neck edge; finish row. Turn work.
   - Work across row. Turn work.

- BO 2 (2, 3) sts at neck edge; finish row. Turn work.
- Cont until front is the same length as back. Place rem sts on a holder.

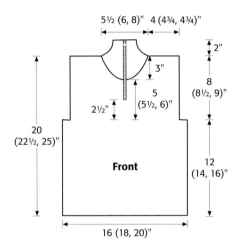

Sleeves

1. With size 10½ needles, CO 23 sts. Work in patt st for 3 rows.

2. Inc 1 st at each end every fourth row 13 (14, 15) times [49 (51, 53) sts].

3. Cont until work measures 14" (15", 16") from bottom.

4. Beg sleeve cap shaping:
   - BO 5 sts at beg of next 2 rows.
   - Work even 2 rows.
   - BO 5 sts at beg of next 6 rows.
   - BO rem 9 (11, 13) sts loosely.

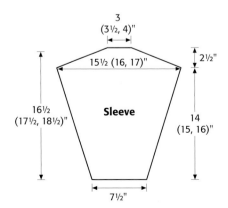

Finishing

1. Join shoulder seams using three-needle bind-off method (see page 18); bind off back neck sts at the same time.

2. With size 10 needle, PU about 55 sts evenly around neck for collar. Make adjustments by increasing or decreasing sts in first row to align rib patt with front and back of sweater.

3. Work in patt st for 2", ending with a WS row.

4. (RS) Purl across row to create a turning row.

5. Work in patt for 2". BO loosely.

6. Zipper opening:
   - Work 1 row sc around zipper opening.
   - Use a backstitch to sew the zipper in by hand.
   - Turn collar to inside along turning row and sew edges to zipper tape. Sew collar to inside along neckline.

7. Sew in sleeve caps. Then sew side seams and sleeve seams.

8. Block the sweater, referring to page 17.

When I'm planning a garment, I like to visualize the whole outfit: how it is going to be worn and with what coordinates. And that often means that I sew skirts or slacks to wear with my sweaters. For this particular design, my idea was to copy the popular fashion trend of pairing a taffeta skirt with a short sweater. To make the outfit easier for my daughter to wear, I simply attached the sweater to the skirt. The bows on the shoulders complete the look by making it age-appropriate.

Sizes

Child's 4 (6, 8, 10)
Finished chest:
28" (30", 32", 33")
Finished length:
32½" (33½", 37", 38")

Karolyn's **Party Dress**

Materials

Yarn A: 3 (4, 4, 5) skeins of Katia Nutria (polyester); each skein is approx 126 yards
[378 (504, 504, 630) yards total]

Yarn B: 1 skein of Jacques Fonty Serpentine (polyester), approx 143 yards

1 yard 60"-wide taffeta

Size 6 needles

Size D crochet hook

Gauge

22 sts and 27 rows = 4" in St st using size 6 needles and yarn A. Use a yarn that
knits to this gauge. Always check gauge before starting sweater to ensure proper fit.

2. Beg left neck shaping:

   - Work first 25 (28, 27, 28) sts and place on holder, BO 19 (19, 26, 27) sts; finish row. Turn work.
   - Work across left shoulder sts. Turn work.
   - BO 3 sts at neck edge; finish row. Turn work.
   - Work across row. Turn work.
   - BO 3 sts at neck edge; finish row. Turn work.
   - Work across row. Turn work.
   - BO 2 sts at neck edge; finish row. Turn work.
   - Cont until shoulder is the same length as back.
   - BO rem sts.

3. Work right neck shaping:

   - Join yarn at neck edge, BO 3 sts; finish row. Turn work.
   - Work across row. Turn work.
   - BO 3 sts at neck edge; finish row. Turn work.
   - Work across row. Turn work.
   - BO 2 sts at neck edge; finish row. Turn work.
   - Cont until shoulder is the same length as back.
   - BO rem sts.

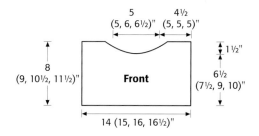

Back

With size 6 needles and yarn A, CO 77 (83, 88, 91) sts. Work in St st for 8" (9", 10½", 11½"). BO loosely.

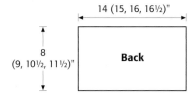

14 (15, 16, 16½)"

8 (9, 10½, 11½)"

Back

Front

1. Work front the same as back until piece measures 6½" (7½", 9", 10"), ending with a WS row.

Sleeves

1. With size 6 needles and yarn A, CO 49 (54, 60, 66) sts. Work in K1, P1 rib for 2 rows.

2. Change to St st and inc 1 st at each end of next row and every fourth row 2 more times [55 (60, 66,72) sts].

3. Work even until sleeve measures 3" (3", 3½", 4"). BO loosely.

```
         10 (11, 12, 13)"
       ┌───────────────┐
3 (3, 3½, 4)" │     Sleeve     │
     └───────────────────┘
          9 (10, 11, 12)"
```

Finishing

1. Sew shoulder seams, referring to page 18.

2. With size D crochet hook and yarn B, work 1 row sc around neckline, then work 1 row rev sc.

3. Sew in sleeves. Sew side seams and under-arm seams.

4. To make bows, cut a 7½" strip crosswise from taffeta fabric. Cut strip in half so you have 2 pieces, each 7½" x 30".

   - Cut a 3"-wide strip from short end of each piece, so you have 2 pieces, each 3" x 7½". Fold strips so 3"-long edges meet in center; press. Fold strips in half again.

   - Fold long bow strips in half lengthwise and sew a ½"-wide seam to make a tube. Turn tubes right side out and press so seams are centered along back.

   - Cut each tube to 18". With right sides together, sew a ½"-wide seam on short ends. Turn.

   - Wrap center of each bow with one of the shorter pieces of taffeta. Wrap bow tight enough to form tucks in bow. Stitch ends of wrap in place by hand; if necessary, cut off any excess wrap fabric. Tack a bow on each shoulder by hand.

5. To make skirt, fold remaining taffeta fabric in half so selvage edges meet. Trim off selvages, then stitch a ½"-wide seam along lengthwise grain. Press seam to one side. Turn up a 4" (4", 2", 2") hem. Sew in place by hand or machine.

6. Gather upper raw edge of skirt to fit lower edge of sweater. Baste to sweater so seam is matched to center back of sweater. Machine stitch waistline seam.

Knitting Terms and Abbreviations

approx	approximately
beg	begin(ning)
BO	bind off
CO	cast on
cont	continue
dec	decrease; decrease by inserting needle into 2 stitches at once and knit (or purl) together as one
garter st	knit every row
inc	increase; increase by working into front and back of the same stitch
K	knit
K2tog	knit 2 stitches together through front loops
MB	make bobble
P	purl
P2tog	purl 2 stitches together through front loops
patt	pattern
psso	pass slip stitch over
PU	pick up
rem	remaining
rep	repeat
rev sc	reverse single crochet (crab stitch)
rib	ribbing; any combination of knits and purls that line up row after row
RS	right side
sc	single crochet
skpo	slip 1 stitch, knit 1 stitch, pass slip stitch over
sl st	slip stitch; slip stitch from left to right needle as if to purl unless specified otherwise
ssk	slip 1, slip 1, then knit the 2 slipped stitches together by inserting the left-hand needle into the front of 2 slipped stitches on the right-hand needle and knit them off together.
st(s)	stitch(es)
St st	stockinette stitch; knit on right-side rows and purl on wrong-side rows
WS	wrong side
wyib	with yarn in back
wyif	with yarn in front
YO	yarn over needle from front to back

Yarn Resources

FOR A LIST of shops in your area that carry the yarns mentioned in this book, call or write the following companies.

CLASSIC ELITE YARNS
300A Jackson Street
Lowell, MA 01854
(978) 453-2837

COLINETTE YARNS
Unique Kolors, Ltd.
1428 Oak Lane
Downington, PA 19335
(800) 252-3934

FILATURA DI CROSA, TAHKI,
AND STACY CHARLES
COLLECTION
1059 Manhattan Avenue
Brooklyn, NY 11222
(800) 962-8008

IRONSTONE YARNS
PO Box 365
Uxbridge, MA 01569
(800) 343-4914

MARKS AND KATTENS YARNS
Swedish Yarn Imports
PO Box 2069
Jamestown, NC 27282
(800) 331-KNIT

RAINBOW MILLS YARNS
5539 Fair Oaks Street
Pittsburgh, PA 15217
(718) 326-5017

REYNOLDS YARNS
JCA, Inc.
35 Scales Lane
Townsend, MA 01469-6340
(800) 225-6340

ROWAN YARNS
Westminster Trading
5 North Boulevard
Amherst, NH 03031
(800) 445-9276

SIRDAR AND KATIA YARNS
Knitting Fever, Inc.
35 Debevoise Avenue
Roosevelt, NY 11575-0502
(800) 645-3457

TRENDSETTER YARNS
Trendsetter
16742 Stagg Street, Unit 104
Van Nuys, CA 91406
(800) 446-2425

WOOL PAK YARNS
Baabajoes Wool Company
1720 Robb Street, 11-103
Lakewood, CO 80215
(303) 239-6313

Bibliography

Bryant, Laura Militzer, and Barry Klein. *Knitting with Novelty Yarns.* Woodinville, Wash.: Martingale & Company, 2001.

Buller, Kate. *The Ultimate Knitter's Guide.* Woodinville, Wash.: Martingale & Company, 2000.

Square, Vicki. *The Knitter's Companion.* Loveland, Colo.: Interweave Press, 1996.

Vogue Knitting. *The Ultimate Knitting Book.* New York: Pantheon Books, 1989.

About the Author

KRISTINE CLEVER received her bachelor of science degree in clothing and textiles from Michigan State University. She has been employed as a fabric-store manager and as an interior designer. She has also owned and operated a custom drapery workroom. Kristine is currently a certified knitting instructor on staff at Crafty Lady in Macomb, Michigan.

Kristine learned to knit when she was six years old, and thirty-something years later she says, "This staple has survived all the phases of my life from college through motherhood, and helped me through life's rough spots. The smooth rhythmic motion has kept me calm and sane, while yarns' color and texture have brought out my creativity. Inspired by the unique qualities of yarn, be it hand or weight, I began designing as a way to blend and emphasize these features."

A portion of the proceeds from the sale of this book is being donated to the Beckwith Wiedemann Support Network, an organization started in 1989 to help families with children affected by this genetic disorder.

new and bestselling titles from

Martingale & COMPANY
America's Best-Loved Craft & Hobby Books™

That Patchwork Place®
America's Best-Loved Quilt Books®

KNITTING & CROCHET
Too Cute
Crochet for Babies and Toddlers
Crocheted Sweaters
Fair Isle Sweaters Simplified
Irresistible Knits
Knit It Your Way
Knitted Shawls, Stoles, and Scarves
Knitting with Novelty Yarns
Paintbox Knits
Simply Beautiful Sweaters
Simply Beautiful Sweaters for Men
The Ultimate Knitter's Guide

NEW RELEASES
All Through the Woods
American Quilt Classics
Amish Wall Quilts
Animal Kingdom CD-ROM
Batik Beauties
The Casual Quilter
Fantasy Floral Quilts
Fast Fusible Quilts
Friendship Blocks
From the Heart
Log Cabin Fever
Machine-Stitched Cathedral Stars
Magical Hexagons
Potting Shed Patchwork
Repliqué Quilts

APPLIQUÉ
Artful Album Quilts
Artful Appliqué
Colonial Appliqué
Red and Green: An Appliqué Tradition
Rose Sampler Supreme

BABY QUILTS
Easy Paper-Pieced Baby Quilts
Even More Quilts for Baby: Easy as ABC
More Quilts for Baby: Easy as ABC
Play Quilts
The Quilted Nursery
Quilts for Baby: Easy as ABC

HOLIDAY QUILTS
Christmas at That Patchwork Place
Holiday Collage Quilts
Paper Piece a Merry Christmas
A Snowman's Family Album Quilt
Welcome to the North Pole

LEARNING TO QUILT
Basic Quiltmaking Techniques for:
    Borders and Bindings
    Divided Circles
    Hand Appliqué
    Machine Appliqué
    Strip Piecing
The Joy of Quilting
The Simple Joys of Quilting
Your First Quilt Book (or it should be!)

SCRAP QUILTS
Nickel Quilts
Scrap Frenzy
Scrappy Duos
Spectacular Scraps

PAPER PIECING
50 Fabulous Paper-Pieced Stars
For the Birds
Paper Piece a Flower Garden
Paper-Pieced Bed Quilts
Paper-Pieced Curves
A Quilter's Ark
Show Me How to Paper Piece

ROTARY CUTTING
101 Fabulous Rotary-Cut Quilts
365 Quilt Blocks a Year Perpetual Calendar
Around the Block Again
Biblical Blocks
Creating Quilts with Simple Shapes
Flannel Quilts
More Fat Quarter Quilts
More Quick Watercolor Quilts
Razzle Dazzle Quilts

CRAFTS
The Art of Stenciling
Baby Dolls and Their Clothes
Creating with Paint
Creepy Crafty Halloween
The Decorated Kitchen
The Decorated Porch
A Handcrafted Christmas
Painted Chairs
Sassy Cats

Our books are available at bookstores and your favorite craft, fabric and yarn retailers. If you don't see the title you're looking for, visit us at www.martingale-pub.com or contact us at:

1-800-426-3126

International: 1-425-483-3313

Fax: 1-425-486-7596

E-mail: info@martingale-pub.com

For more information and a full list of our titles, visit our
Web site or call for a free catalog.
